THIS JOURNAL BELONGS TO:

CREATIVE NOTEBOOKS

We would love to hear from you! Connect with us at:

✉ info@creativenotebooks.com

↖ www.creativenotebooks.com

ⓕ facebook.com/creativenotebooks

⊙ instagram.com/creative.notebooks

73853220R00086